CH

Recipes

compiled by
Simon Haseltine

illustrated with nostalgic childhood scenes by
Trevor Mitchell

SALMON

Index

Printed and published by J. Salmon Ltd., Sevenoaks, England

Getting Started

Baking your own cakes and biscuits is great fun and it is wonderful to eat home-made food which you have cooked yourself. Read the tips on this page carefully for successful and safe baking.

Preparation

Read through the recipe carefully before you start baking. Wash your hands thoroughly and wear an apron. Assemble all the ingredients and equipment which you will need.

Safety in the Kitchen

Always ask an adult to supervise you at all times. Use oven gloves when handling hot dishes or baking tins. Take care when using sharp knives or utensils and when handling saucepans on a hot cooker. Always hold the handle if stirring food and be careful not to put hot pans directly onto a work surface.

Measuring

Carefully measure all ingredients. The quantities needed are shown in metric and imperial measurements.

Cooking Times

Use the middle shelf of the oven (unless the recipe says otherwise), and, if you have a fan oven, you may need to reduce the temperature or cooking time slightly.

Storage

If you want to keep your cakes or biscuits for later, cool them thoroughly and then store in a sealed, airtight container.

Ginger Fairings

A wonderful old-fashioned crunchy biscuit which children would buy with their pocket money at the fairgrounds in the West Country.

100g (3½ oz.) margarine
225g (8 oz.) self-raising flour
Pinch bicarbonate of soda
1 level tsp. ginger
1 level tsp. mixed spice
100g (3½ oz.) caster sugar
2 tsp. golden syrup

Preheat the oven to 190°C (375°F) or Mark 5. Melt the margarine and syrup together in a saucepan over a gentle heat. Sift the dry ingredients together, then add to the melted margarine and syrup mixture and mix well. Turn the dough out of the pan and roll into 16 small walnut-sized balls with your hands. Place on a greased baking tray and bake in the oven for around 12 minutes, or until golden brown. Makes 16 biscuits.

Yoghurt Pot Muffins

Children can choose their favourite yoghurt,
and then use the pot to make these delicious muffins.

1 small pot yoghurt (choose your favourite flavour)
¾ pot sunflower oil   1 pot caster sugar
3 pots self-raising flour   1 tsp. baking powder
1 pot dried fruit/chopped fresh fruit
1 egg (beaten)   ½ pot milk

Preheat the oven to 180°C (350°F) or Mark 4. Empty the chosen yoghurt into a mixing bowl and keep the pot to measure out the remaining ingredients. Add the oil to the bowl, then the egg and milk and mix thoroughly. Next, add the sugar and mix before adding the flour and baking powder. Finally, fold in the fruit. Dollop the mixture into paper muffin cases and bake for 20 to 25 minutes, or until golden brown and springy on top. Makes 12 muffins.

Cheesy Muffins

Lovely served hot with lashings of butter straight from the oven or cold on the lawn…

2 cups of grated mature Cheddar cheese
1½ cups self-raising flour 1 tbsp. sugar
Pinch of English mustard powder
1 egg 1 cup milk Pinch dried herbs
1 rasher bacon

Preheat the oven to 200°C (400°F) or Mark 6. First, grill the bacon and allow to cool before chopping into small pieces. Next, mix the egg and milk together in a small bowl. Place all the remaining ingredients (including the cooked bacon pieces) into a large bowl and mix to combine well. Add the egg and milk and fold in gently. Spoon the mixture into 12 muffin cases and bake for around 15 minutes until golden brown. Makes 12 muffins.

Rocky Road Refrigerator Cake

You can have fun "baking" this cake in the fridge!

450g (1 lb.) bar milk chocolate
1 tin of condensed milk
100g (3½ oz.) butter
Bag of small marshmallows
Small tub of glacé cherries
Handful chopped nuts
Packet of digestive biscuits
Handful (in total) raisins and sultanas

Put the digestive biscuits in a thick plastic bag and roughly crush with a rolling pin until they form chunky biscuit pieces. In a saucepan, melt the chocolate and butter together over a low heat, then add the condensed milk, mixing thoroughly. Take the chocolate mixture off the heat and mix in the digestive biscuits, cherries, marshmallows, nuts and fruit. Tip the mixture into a tin lined with cling film, flatten out and score into squares with a sharp knife. Place in the fridge to set. Makes 12 squares.

Gingerbread Men

The wonderful smell when baking these gingerbread men will fill your kitchen…

350g (12 oz.) plain flour
2 tsp. ground ginger
1 tsp. bicarbonate of soda
100g (3½ oz.) butter
175g (6 oz.) soft light brown sugar
1 egg (beaten)
4 tbsp. golden syrup
White icing (to decorate)

Preheat the oven to 190°C (375°F) or Mark 5 and grease two baking trays. Put the flour, ginger and bicarbonate of soda into a large bowl and rub in the butter. Add the sugar and then stir in the syrup and egg to make a firm dough. Roll out to about 5mm (¼ inch) thick and cut out your gingerbread men using a gingerbread cutter. Place each gingerbread man on the baking trays and bake for 10 to 15 minutes until golden brown. Leave to cool slightly before placing on a wire rack.Once cold, decorate with white icing. Makes about 20 biscuits (depending on cutter size).

Trevor Mitchell

Oaty Biscuits

You can "hob-nob" with your friends with these delicious biscuits!

75g (2½ oz.) plain flour
½ tsp. bicarbonate of soda
75g (2½ oz.) demerara sugar
75g (2½ oz.) porridge oats
75g (2½ oz.) butter
1 tbsp. golden syrup

Preheat the oven to 170°C (325°F) or Mark 3. Put the plain flour in a bowl with the bicarbonate of soda. Add the demerara sugar and porridge oats and stir together. Melt the butter in a pan with the golden syrup, then add to the dry ingredients and mix well together. Take handfuls of the mixture and roll into around 24 small balls. Set them well apart on a greased baking tray and flatten slightly. Bake for around 15 minutes until golden brown and leave to cool on a wire rack. Makes 24 biscuits.

No Baking Rice Krispie Cakes

An old-fashioned recipe which children will remember and bake with their own in years to come…

3 cups Rice Krispies **1 tbsp. sugar**
4 tbsp. golden syrup **1 tbsp. butter**
Few drops of vanilla essence

Put syrup, sugar and butter into a pan and melt gently, then bring to the boil for 1 minute, stirring all the time. Remove from the heat and add the vanilla essence and Rice Krispies. Fold in well and then dollop the mixture into 12 cake cases in a bun tin. Put in the fridge to set. Makes 12 cakes.

Trevor Mitchell

Easter Bunny Biscuits

Design your own Easter Bunny eggs…

85g (3 oz.) butter   85g (3 oz.) caster sugar
Rind of 1 lemon (finely grated)
175g (6 oz.) plain flour   ½ tsp. mixed spice
60g (2 oz.) currants   1 egg (beaten)
Icing and mini chocolate eggs to decorate

Preheat oven to 190°C (375°F) or Mark 5 and grease a baking tray. Cream the butter and sugar until pale, then add the lemon rind. Next, fold in the flour, mixed spice, currants and egg to form a stiff dough. Roll out the biscuit dough to 1cm (½ inch) thick and with a biscuit cutter, cut out the bunny shapes. Carefully place each biscuit on the baking tray using a palette knife and bake for around 10 minutes until golden brown. Place on a wire rack to cool, then decorate with coloured icing and mini eggs. Makes around 18 biscuits.

Cupcakes

We all love cupcakes, especially if we can ice and decorate them with our own tasty designs…

Cupcake:

100g (3½ oz.) unsalted butter (softened) 100g (3½ oz.) self-raising flour
100g (3½ oz.) caster sugar 2 eggs

Cream cheese frosting:

300g (10½ oz.) icing sugar 50g (1¾ oz.) softened unsalted butter
125g (4½ oz.) cream cheese Plus a selection of small sweets for decoration

Preheat the oven to 180°C (350°F) or Mark 4. In a large bowl, whisk all the cupcake ingredients until creamy. Spoon into individual cupcake cases and bake in the oven for around 10 to 15 minutes until golden brown. Place on a wire rack to cool. Meanwhile, to make the frosting, put the icing sugar and butter in a bowl and beat together until well mixed. Add the cream cheese and whisk until the frosting is light and fluffy. Spread onto the cold cupcakes with a flat knife or pipe on using a piping bag. Finally, add a selection of small sweets as decoration. To change the colour of the frosting, add a drop or two of food colouring. To make chocolate cupcakes, replace 20g (¾ oz.) of flour with cocoa powder. Makes 12 cupcakes.

Gluten, Nut and Dairy Free Chocolate Brownies

A "free for all"...

50g (1¾ oz.) gluten-free and dairy-free dark chocolate
100g (3½ oz.) dairy-free margarine 200g (7 oz.) caster sugar
2 eggs (lightly whisked) 2 tsp. vanilla extract
75g (2½ oz.) gluten-free flour
½ tsp. gluten-free baking powder

Preheat the oven to 180°C (350°F) or Mark 4, then grease and line an 8 inch square tin with baking parchment. Gently melt the chocolate in a small saucepan. In a large bowl, cream the margarine and sugar until pale, then beat in the eggs, vanilla extract and melted chocolate. Lastly, stir in the flour and baking powder. Spread the mixture in the tin and bake in the oven for around 30 minutes. Leave to cool, then cut into squares. Makes 12 squares.

Fruity Flapjacks

Fruity flapjacks are a favourite with children, especially homemade ones in their lunch boxes.

50g (1¾ oz.) ready to eat dried prunes (chopped)
50g (1¾ oz.) ready to eat dried apricots (chopped)
50g (1¾ oz.) (in total) raisins and sultanas (or other dried fruit)
175g (6 oz.) porridge oats 50g (1¾ oz.) butter
3 tbsp. clear honey
1 egg (beaten)

Preheat the oven to 180°C (350°F) or Mark 4 and lightly grease a small shallow (9 x 7 inch) baking tray. Place the prunes, apricots, raisins, sultanas and oats into a mixing bowl and stir to combine. In a small saucepan, melt the butter with the honey and add to the fruit and oats, mixing well. Allow to cool then add the beaten egg and fold through. Turn the mixture into the greased tray and level the surface. Place in the oven and bake for 15 to 20 minutes until a pale golden brown. Leave in the tin until almost cold and then score into fingers with a sharp knife. Remove from the tin to finish cooling on a wire rack. Can be stored in an airtight container for a few days. Makes 12 flapjacks.

TM Coaches
SCHOOLS
LTA 901

Iced Biscuits

The kids will love baking these little biscuits and then making up their own decorations.

100g (3½ oz.) unsalted butter (softened) 100g (3½ oz.) caster sugar
1 egg (lightly beaten) 275g (9½ oz.) plain flour 1 tsp. vanilla extract

To decorate:
450g (1 lb.) icing sugar 3 tbsp. water 2 drops food colouring (or use various colours)

Preheat the oven to 190°C (375°F) or Mark 5 and line a baking tray with greaseproof paper. Next, cream the butter and sugar together in a bowl, then add the egg and vanilla extract, a little at a time, until well combined. Stir in the flour until the mixture comes together as a dough and roll out on a lightly floured work surface to a thickness of a pound coin. Using a selection of biscuit cutters, cut biscuits out of the dough and carefully place them onto the baking tray (using a palette knife helps). Bake in the oven for around 10 minutes, or until pale golden brown. Remove from the oven and set aside to harden for 5 minutes, then cool on a wire rack. Meanwhile, to make the icing, sift the icing sugar into a large mixing bowl and stir in enough water to create a smooth mixture, then stir in the chosen food colouring. Carefully spread the icing onto the cold biscuits using a knife and set aside until the icing hardens. Makes around 18 biscuits.

Giant Party Cookies

Bake these, then decorate and write your guest's name on them for birthday place settings...

250g (9 oz.) butter (unsalted) softened (plus extra for greasing)
250g (9 oz.) unrefined golden caster sugar 2 eggs (lightly beaten)
1 tsp. vanilla extract 1 level tsp. baking powder
500g (1¼ lb.) plain flour (plus extra for dusting)

Preheat the oven to 170°C (325°F) or Mark 3 and baking tray with greased parchment paper. Beat together the butter and sugar in a large bowl until light and fluffy. Next, beat in the eggs and vanilla extract. Sift together the flour and baking powder in a separate bowl and stir into the butter mixture, working into a dough using floured hands. Turn onto a floured surface and knead into a ball and divide in two. Wrap in cling film and chill in the fridge for 1 hour. Place half the dough on a floured surface and dust with a little more flour. Roll out to the thickness of a pound coin and cut out the round shapes. Place slightly apart on the baking tray and cook for around 10 minutes or until lightly coloured. Cool on a rack. Repeat until all the dough is used. Now the fun bit – use a selection of small sweets and icing to decorate your cookies and then write your guest's name on (see recipe). Makes around 12 cookies.

POST OFFICE
AND
VILLAGE STORE
LYONS
CAKES
TELEPHONE
ER
Trevor Mitchell

Birthday Name Place Cookies

Wonderful for the children to create using homemade or shop-bought cookies for their birthday party.

250g (8¾ oz.) icing sugar
½ tsp. peppermint extract
A little cold water
4 giant cookies (see Giant Party Cookie recipe in this book, but fun with shop bought too)
Selection of small sweets and sprinkles to decorate
Icing pen

Mix the icing sugar with a little peppermint extract and enough water to make a thick icing. Spread the icing over cookies and create a border around the edges using a selection of small colourful sweets and sprinkles. Leave for 15 minutes for the icing to set. Then, using an icing pen, write your guest's name in the centre of each cookie. When the icing is dry, wrap in cellophane to keep crispy and tie with a ribbon. Enough for around 6 giant cookies.

Cheesy Sticks

Make and serve these tasty cheesy sticks with a variety of dips for a special teatime treat…

4 sheets puff pastry
1 egg (lightly beaten)
30ml. (1 fl.oz.) milk
3 cups Cheddar cheese (grated)

Preheat the oven to 180°C (350°F) or Mark 4. Mix the milk and egg together and brush over one surface of each pastry sheet. Next, sprinkle the grated cheese equally over the egg wash on two of the pastry sheets and cover with the other two sheets, pressing flat. Cut into eight strips of equal size and place on the baking tray. Pick up and twist each strip and then brush with the remaining egg wash. Bake on a greased baking tray for 10 to 15 minutes until golden brown. Leave to cool on a wire rack. Makes around 16 cheesy sticks.

Bread Rolls

Bread rolls are easy and great fun for children to make…

425g (15 oz.) strong white/wholemeal/granary bread flour (in any combination)
Plus extra flour for dusting

2 tbsp. olive oil	**1¼ tsp. fast action dried yeast**
1½ tsp. honey	**260ml. (⅓ pint) warm water**
½ tsp. salt	**3 tsp. mixed seeds**

Put the flour into a large bowl, add oil and mix well. Next, stir in the honey, salt and yeast. Make a well and add enough of the water to form a soft dough. Knead the dough on a floured work surface for 5 minutes and then cover and put aside in a warm place to rise for around 60 minutes. Knead again and cut the dough into 12 chunks and roll into bread rolls. Place on a greased baking tray, cover and leave to rise for a further 30 minutes. Bake in the oven for 10 to 15 minutes, until hollow sounding when tapped on the bottom, then turn out and cool on a wire rack. Makes 12 rolls.

Cheese and Bacon Rolls

Easy to make and totally scrummy to eat…

2 packets of dried yeast (7g (¼ oz.) each) 1 tsp. sugar 1½ cups of warm water
5 cups plain flour 2 tsp. salt ½ cup milk 2 tbsp. sugar
60g (2 oz.) butter (melted) 1 egg (beaten) 1 tbsp. milk
1 cup Cheddar cheese (grated) 6 bacon rashers (fried and chopped)

Preheat oven to 180°C (350°F) or Mark 4 and cover a baking tray with greaseproof paper and set aside. Combine the yeast, sugar and water in a small bowl and stir until dissolved. Leave in a warm place for 10 minutes or until it becomes frothy. Sift the flour and salt into a large mixing bowl and then stir in the yeast mixture, milk, sugar and melted butter. Mix with your hands to form a soft dough. Knead on a floured board for around 5 minutes then place in a greased bowl, cover with cling film and leave in a warm place for at least 30 minutes until it has doubled in size. Turn out on a floured board, sprinkle over the bacon bits and grated cheese, then knead again for a further 5 minutes, folding in well. Divide into 12 and roll each portion into a thick sausage shape. Place on a greased tray, cover with cling film and leave to rise for 15 minutes. Meanwhile, mix the milk and beaten egg together and brush over the risen pastry. Bake in the oven for around 20 minutes until golden brown. Serve warm. Makes 12 rolls.

MINOR
1000
Trevor Mitchell

Grandma's Butterfly Cakes

An old-fashioned recipe which I baked in my grandma's kitchen years ago…

For the cakes:

2 eggs 110g (3¾ oz.) self-raising flour 110g (3¾ oz.) butter
110g (3¾ oz.) caster sugar 2 tsp. baking powder

For the icing:

220g (7¾ oz.) icing sugar (plus extra for sprinkling)
110g (3¾ oz.) butter Dash of milk

Preheat the oven to 200°C (400°F) or Mark 6 and place 12 cake cases in a bun tin. Mix the sugar, flour and baking powder together in a large bowl, then add the butter and eggs. Whisk the mixture well until combined. Using a small spoon, fill the cake cases with the mixture and bake in the oven for around 15 minutes or until they are golden brown. When cooked, remove from the oven and place on a cooling rack. Meanwhile, to make the icing, whisk the butter and half the sugar together, then mix in the remaining sugar and a dash of milk, continue whisking until thick and creamy. Take each cake and, using a sharp knife, cut an upside-down, shallow bowl shape out the top of each cake, and then cut this disc in half to form the two butterfly wings. Fill the hole in the cake with the icing and then stick the wings in the icing to form wings. Sprinkle some icing sugar over the top of the cakes. Makes 12 cakes.

Strawberry Meringues

Homemade sticky meringues, glued together with thick cream and sliced strawberries…

4 large egg whites (room temperature)
115g (4 oz.) caster sugar 115g (4 oz.) icing sugar
Small tub double cream (whipped)
12 strawberries (halved)

Preheat the oven to a cool 110°C (230°F) or Mark ¼ and line two baking sheets with parchment paper. Put the egg whites into a large clean and dry mixing bowl and beat them on medium speed with an electric hand whisk until the mixture stands up in stiff peaks. Next, add the caster sugar, a little at a time. Continue beating for a few seconds between each addition until thick and glossy. Sift one third of the icing sugar over the mixture, then gently fold it in with a big metal spoon. Continue to sift and fold in the remaining icing sugar a third at a time until smooth. Scoop up a heaped dessertspoonful of the meringue and place on to the baking sheet to make 12 oval shapes. Bake for around 1½ hours until the meringues sound crisp when tapped underneath and are a pale coffee colour. Leave to cool on a cooling rack. Serve two meringues sandwiched together with a dollop of whipped double cream and some halved strawberries. Makes around 6 meringues.

DUBLO
Trevor
Mitchell

Lemon Star Decorations

Festive and edible Christmas tree decorations which will delight your children…

325g (11½ oz.) plain flour 200g (7 oz.) chilled salted butter (small chunks)
125g (4½ oz.) golden caster sugar 2 tsp. vanilla extract 2 egg yolks
100g (3½ oz.) dried fruits (use mangoes, pineapple and papaya – all chopped)
50g (1¾ oz.) dried cranberries (chopped) 2 tbsp. lemon juice 200g (7 oz.) icing sugar
Small handful silver balls Ribbon (for hanging on the tree)

Preheat the oven to 180°C (350°F) or Mark 4 and grease two large baking sheets. To make the biscuit, sieve the flour into a large mixing bowl and add the butter. Rub the butter into the flour with your fingers until the mixture looks like breadcrumbs. Add the remaining ingredients and mix until the mixture forms a dough. Roll out the dough to a thickness of about 5mm (¼ inch) and cut out star biscuits using a 10cm (4 inch) cutter. With a sharp skewer, make a small hole 1cm (½ inch) from a single point on each star. Bake for around 20 minutes until turning pale golden around the edges, then transfer to a wire rack to cool. Meanwhile, to make the decoration, put the icing sugar in a bowl and beat in the lemon juice to make a smooth icing. Using a small palette knife, spread the icing over the cold biscuits but leave the edges plain. Mix the fruits, then scatter them in the middle of the icing together with some silver balls. Leave for at least 2 hours to set. Thread with ribbon through the pre-made hole just before you hang them and eat within 24 hours. Makes around 18 biscuits.

Hot Cross Buns

Hot cross buns, hot cross buns, one a penny, two a penny, hot cross buns...

450g (1 lb.) strong plain flour 1½ tsp. fast-action dried yeast 200ml (7 fl.oz.) milk
½ tsp. of salt 1 level tsp. mixed spice 75g (2½ oz.) caster sugar
50g (1¾ oz.) butter (melted) 1 egg 50g (1¾ oz.) dried mixed fruit

Glaze: 40g (1½ oz.) caster sugar 2 tbsp. boiling water

Preheat the oven to 200°C (400°F) or Mark 6 and grease two baking trays. Put all the dry ingredients, including the yeast into a bowl and stir in the melted butter. Next, mix together the egg and milk in a separate bowl and then gradually mix into the dried ingredients, a little at a time, to form a dough. Knead well until you have a smooth but not sticky dough, adding a little more flour or water if needed. Next, place the dough into a bowl, cover with cling film, and leave in a warm place to rise for an hour. Place the dough back on a floured surface and knead for a few minutes, then divide into 12 and shape each into buns. Set the buns well apart on the prepared trays, cover and leave in a warm place until doubled in size. Make two cuts on the top of each bun to form a cross and bake for around 20 minutes or until golden brown. Remove from the oven and cool on a wire rack. Dissolve the icing sugar in the boiling water to make the glaze and brush over the buns whilst they are still warm. Serve toasted with lashings of butter. Makes 12 buns.

Triple Chocolate Cookies

Children will love these Triple Chocolate Cookies – three times the yumminess!

125g (4½ oz.) light muscovado sugar   125g (4½ oz.) butter
150g (5¼ oz.) porridge oats   1 egg
125g (4½ oz.) wholemeal plain flour
100g (3½ oz.) (in total) of milk, dark and white chocolate pieces

Heat the oven to 180°C (350°F) or Mark 4 and grease two baking trays. In a bowl, cream the sugar and butter together, then add the porridge oats and egg and mix well. Sieve in the wholemeal flour, then add the chocolate pieces and mix together. Lastly, divide the mixture into six and, using your hands, roll into balls. Place on the baking trays well apart, then flatten them with the palms of your hands. Bake in the middle of the oven for 15 minutes or until golden brown. Leave to cool on a wire rack. Makes 6 large cookies.

Festive Mince Pies

These delicious mince pies are not just for Christmas…

225g (8 oz.) cold butter (diced)
350g (12¼ oz.) plain flour
100g (3½ oz.) golden caster sugar
280g (10 oz.) mincemeat
1 egg
Icing sugar (to dust)

Preheat the oven to 200°C (400°F) or Mark 6. First, rub the butter into the flour, then mix in the caster sugar and a pinch of salt. Combine the pastry into a ball and knead until firm. Divide the dough into two (one slightly larger than the other). With the larger ball of dough, cut out with a large pastry cutter into 18 discs and line the holes of two 12-hole patty tins. Next, spoon the mincemeat into the pies, then take the remaining dough, roll out and cut lids with a smaller pastry cutter to cover the pies. Top the pies with their lids, pressing the edges gently together to seal. Beat the egg and brush the tops of the pies. Bake for 20 minutes until golden. Leave to cool in the tin for 5 minutes, then remove to a wire rack. To serve, lightly dust with icing sugar. Makes 18 little pies.

Gluten Free Fruity Muffins

Have fun choosing your ingredients for this delicious muffin…

1 egg
½ cup fruit juice
2 tbsp. granulated sugar
2 tbsp. vegetable oil
1 cup brown rice flour
2 tsp. gluten-free baking powder
¼ tsp. salt
2 tbsp. chopped nuts (optional – leave out if nut free)
¾ cup fresh fruit (try blueberries, raspberries, finely chopped apples or peaches)

Preheat oven to 220°C (425°F) or Mark 7 and line the muffin tray with muffin cases. In large mixing bowl, combine the egg, fruit juice, sugar and oil, beating in a food mixer on low speed until smooth. In another bowl, combine the rice flour, baking powder and salt. Add to the egg mixture and beat on low until combined. Gently fold in the nuts (if using) and fruit pieces. Divide the batter among the muffin cases and bake for 15 minutes or until golden brown on top. Make 6 muffins.

Banana Flapjacks

Banana flavoured flapjacks – perfect for a long family walk on a sunny day…

200g (7 oz.) butter
350g (12 oz.) soft brown sugar
3½ tbsp. golden syrup
450g (1 lb.) rolled oats
1 banana

Preheat the oven to 180°C (350°F) or Mark 4 and grease and line a shallow baking tray. Put the butter, brown sugar and golden syrup into a saucepan and melt together on a medium heat. Then mash the banana and add to the melted butter. Now, add the oats and stir through the mixture to ensure they are well covered. Spoon the mixture into the baking tray and bake for 25 minutes, or until the top is brown. Cool slightly, then cut into 14 fingers. Makes 14 flapjacks.

POST OFFICE AND VILLAGE STORE
LYONS CAKES
TELEPHONE
FIREWORKS ON SALE HERE
FJC 80
Trevor Mitchell

Saucy Sausage Rolls

A quick and easy sausage roll to make – and they come with their own tomato ketchup too!

6 sausages (good quality)   1 onion (finely diced)
1 tsp. dried herbs   1 handful of breadcrumbs
250g (8¾ oz.) puff pastry   1 egg mixed with 1 tbsp. of milk (to glaze)
Glug of tomato ketchup   Oil (for frying)
Plain flour (for dusting)

Preheat the oven to 200°C (400°F) or Mark 6. In a frying pan, sauté the diced onion in a little oil and then add the herbs. Stir through and set aside to cool. Split open your sausages and pop the sausage meat filling in a bowl, then mix in the breadcrumbs and the cooled onions. Roll out your pastry on a surface dusted with flour to a thickness of 3mm then cut into two long rectangles. Now, roll the sausage meat mix into two long sausage shapes and line along the centre of each pastry rectangle. Paint a little of the eggmix on the edges and fold the pastry over the sausage filling. Pinch together the outside edge with your fingers to seal and cut into sausage roll lengths. Place on a baking tray and then brush the egg/milk mix on the outside of each. Place in the oven for 25 minutes until golden brown and puffed up. Makes 4 large or 8 small sausage rolls.

Cheesy Garlic Bread

A scrummy homemade garlic bread ideal for a warming chilli con carne…

500g (1¼ lb.) strong white bread flour
7g (¼ oz.) sachet fast-action yeast
1 tsp. salt
½ pt. water (warm)
2 tbsp. olive oil
1 tbsp. clear honey
2 garlic cloves (crushed)
25g (¾ oz.) butter (softened)
100g (3½ oz.) mature Cheddar (grated)
Pinch dried mixed herbs
Plain flour (for dusting)

Preheat the oven to 200°C (400°F) or Mark 6 and grease a Swiss roll tray. First, sieve the flour, yeast and salt into a large bowl. Next, mix the water with the oil and honey in a small bowl, then pour into the dry mix, stirring all the time to form a soft dough. Turn the dough out onto a dusted floured surface, then knead for 5 minutes. Now stretch the dough to fit the Swiss roll tin. Mix the garlic with the butter, then dot over the dough. Next, sprinkle over the grated cheese and mixed herbs. Cover the garlic bread with lightly oiled cling film, then leave in a warm place to rise for around 50 minutes. Remove the cling film, then bake the bread for around 30 minutes until golden and risen. Leave to cool slightly then cut into 12 pieces and serve. Makes 12 squares.

Blackberry and Apple Tray Bake

A simple-to-make fruity tray bake which can be served on a picnic or as a teatime treat…

225g (8 oz.) butter (softened – plus extra for greasing)

350g (12¼ oz.) cooking apples	**4 eggs**
125g (4½ oz.) blackberries	**2 tsp. vanilla extract**
Juice of ½ lemon	**350g (12¼ oz.) self-raising flour**
280g (10 oz.) golden caster sugar	**2 tsp. baking powder**

Demerara sugar (to sprinkle)

Preheat the oven to 180°C (350°F) or Mark 4 and butter and line a rectangular baking tin (10½ in x 7¾ in) with parchment paper. Now, peel, core and thinly slice the apples, place in a bowl and squeeze the lemon juice over them. Next, place the butter, caster sugar, eggs, vanilla, flour and baking powder into a large bowl and mix until smooth. Spread half the mixture into the prepared tin. Arrange half the apples over the top of the mixture, then repeat the layers. Scatter over the blackberries on top and gently poke them into the batter. Finally, sprinkle over the demerara sugar. Bake for around 50 minutes until golden brown. Leave to cool for 10 minutes, then turn out and cut into squares. Cuts into 16 pieces.

Strawberry Jam and Lemon Curd Tarts

A delightful plate of colourful red and yellow tarts…

250g (8¾ oz.) plain flour
Pinch of salt
100g (3½ oz.) butter (cubed)
3 tbsp. cold water
Jars of strawberry jam and lemon curd
Butter for greasing

Preheat the oven to 180°C (350°F) or Mark 4 and grease a 12-hole tart mould with a little butter. Place the flour, butter and salt into a large bowl and rub the butter into the flour with your fingertips until the mixture resembles fine breadcrumbs. Add the water to the mixture and using a cold knife stir until the dough binds together, adding a little more water if the mixture is too dry. Wrap the dough in clingfilm and chill in the fridge for 15 minutes. Place the cold dough onto a floured board and roll out to the thickness of a penny coin. Using a tart cutter, cut circles from the pastry and gently press into each hole. Finally, dollop a heaped teaspoon of jam or lemon curd into the pastry tarts. Bake in the oven for around 15 minutes or until golden brown. Remove from the oven and leave to cool completely. Serve colourfully arranged on a plate with a glass of lemonade. Makes 12 tarts.

Trevor Mitchell

Chewy Cereal Bars

A taste of nature, healthy, sweet and moist…

2 tbsp. sunflower seeds 2 tbsp. pumpkin seeds
2 tbsp. linseeds 2 bananas
100g (3½ oz.) unsalted butter (plus extra for greasing)
3 tbsp. golden syrup 2 oz. cornflakes 100g (3½ oz.) rolled oats
100g (3½ oz.) stoned dried dates (roughly chopped)

Preheat the oven to 180°C (350°F) or Mark 4, grease a 11 × 7 × 1½ inch cake tin and line the bottom with greased baking parchment. Roughly chop the sunflower seeds, pumpkin seeds and linseeds, then peel and mash the bananas. Melt the butter in a saucepan and stir in the golden syrup. Add the chopped seeds and mashed bananas, together with the cornflakes, rolled oats and dates. Mix together well, then spoon into the cake tin and level the surface. Bake for around 30 minutes or until golden brown. Leave to cool in the tin for 5 minutes, then score into 14 bars. Once cold, remove from the tin and separate the bars. Keep in an airtight tin for up to two days. Makes 14 bars.

Rhubarb and Lemon Curd Cake

A celebratory cake, ideal for Mother's Day, but child's play to make…

225g (8 oz.) unsalted butter (softened, plus extra for greasing)   225g (8 oz.) caster sugar
Zest 1 lemon   4 eggs (beaten)   75g (2½ oz.) ground almonds
200g (7 oz.) self-raising flour   140g (5 oz.) rhubarb (chunks)   1 tbsp. demerara sugar
75ml (2½ fl.oz.) double cream   3 tbsp. lemon curd (plus extra for drizzling)   A little water

Preheat the oven to 180°C (350°F) or Mark 4 and lightly butter a deep, round 20cm (8 inch) cake tin and line the base with a circle of greased baking parchment. Place the butter in a large bowl and beat until light and fluffy, then add the caster sugar and lemon zest and beat again. Gradually add the eggs to the mixture until fully combined. Stir in the ground almonds, then the flour, and fold together using a large spoon. Next, fold through half the rhubarb, then transfer the mixture into the prepared cake tin and scatter over the remaining rhubarb. Finish with the demerara sugar sprinkled over the top. Bake for 45 minutes, or until a skewer inserted into the middle comes out clean. Cool on a wire rack, then remove from the tin. When the cake is cold, make the topping. Whip the cream in a large bowl until it forms soft peaks. In a small bowl, mix the lemon curd with about 1 tbsp. water and carefully fold it through the cream. Spread over the cake, drizzle with a little more lemon curd and serve immediately. Serves 6.

42051
TAXI
CHESTER
ATION MASTER
ROYAL MAIL
ER
Trevor Mitchell

Easy Treacle Sponge

My favourite as a child and far yummier than shop made!

250g (8¾ oz.) golden syrup
1 lemon (zest), plus juice from half the lemon
5 tbsp. breadcrumbs   200g (7 oz.) butter (softened)
200g (7 oz.) golden caster sugar   3 eggs
200g (7 oz.) self-raising flour   5 tbsp. milk

Preheat the oven to 180°C (350°F) or Mark 4. First, mix the golden syrup, lemon zest, juice and breadcrumbs together and spread over the base of a 1½ litre baking tray. Next, beat the butter and sugar until pale and fluffy, then beat in the eggs, one by one. Stir in the flour and milk and dollop over the syrup mixture. Bake for around 40 minutes until golden and risen. Serve with ice cream. Serves 8.

Easy Iced Buns

Children will love baking these old-fashioned iced buns…

500g (1¼ lb.) packet white bread mix (complete mix which contains yeast)
100g (3½ oz.) caster sugar 1 egg 250ml (⅓ pint) water (tepid)
A little flour (for dusting)
350g (12¼ oz.) icing sugar (plus pink food colouring)
A little extra water Sprinkles

Mix together the bread mix and sugar and then add the egg and the tepid water until a soft dough is formed. Knead on a lightly floured surface for around 5 minutes and then place in an oiled bowl, cover with cling film and leave in a warm place for 1 hour until doubled in size. Then remove from the bowl to the floured surface and knock back the dough for a minute or so. Divide into 20 chunks and shape each into a sausage shape and place on an oiled baking tray. Cover with oiled cling film and allow to rise until doubled in size. Meanwhile, preheat the oven to 200°C (400°F) or Mark 6. Remove the cling film and bake the buns for around 10 minutes or until golden. Cool on a wire rack. To decorate, mix the icing sugar with a little water until stiff but spreadable, then add the food colouring. Spread along the top of each bun and scatter with sprinkles. Makes 20 buns.

Love-Heart Lollipop Cookies

Homemade heart-shaped cookies on a stick – perfect for a young Valentine...

1½ cups caster sugar   1 cup unsalted butter   1 egg
2 tsp. vanilla extract   2½ cups plain flour (plus extra for dusting)
1 tsp. baking powder   ½ tsp. salt
Bundle wooden lollipop sticks

To glaze:
2¼ cups icing sugar   2 tbsp. glucose syrup   2 tbsp. milk   Drop of food colouring

Cream the butter and sugar in a bowl until light and fluffy. Then beat in the egg and vanilla, followed by the flour, baking powder and salt to form a dough. Place the dough in a bowl, cover in cling film, and refrigerate for 1 hour. Meanwhile, preheat oven to 190°C (375°F) or Mark 5 and line a baking sheet with baking paper. Remove the dough from the fridge to a floured surface and roll out to the thickness of a pound coin. Cut with a heart-shaped cookie cutter and place each cookie on the tray. Insert a lollipop stick into the base of each cookie, patting down any dough with your fingers. Bake for 10 minutes, or until pale golden. Transfer the cookies to a wire rack to cool. To make the glaze, mix together the icing sugar, syrup and milk, then add a drop of food colouring. Spread over the cold cookies to decorate. Makes around 12 to 18 cookies.

METRIC CONVERSIONS

The weights, measures and oven temperatures used in the preceding recipes can be easily converted to their metric equivalents. The conversions listed below are only approximate, having been rounded up or down as may be appropriate.

Weights

Avoirdupois	Metric
1 oz.	just under 30 grams
4 oz. (¼ lb.)	app. 115 grams
225g (8 oz.) (½ lb.)	app. 230 grams
400g (1 lb.)	454 grams

Liquid Measures

Imperial	Metric
1 tablespoon (liquid only)	20 millilitres
1 fl. oz.	app. 30 millilitres
1 gill (¼ pt.)	app. 145 millilitres
½ pt.	app. 285 millilitres
1 pt.	app. 570 millilitres
1 qt.	app. 1.140 litres

Oven Temperatures

	°Fahrenheit	Gas Mark	°Celsius
Slow	300	2	150
	325	3	170
Moderate	350	4	180
	375	5	190
	400	6	200
Hot	425	7	220
	450	8	230
	475	9	240